SkillAbilities
FOR YOUTH MINISTRY

Caring From the Inside Out

How to Help Youth Show Compassion

by Soozung Sa

ABINGDON PRESS
Nashville, Tennessee

About the Writer

Soozung Sa is a youth director/Christian education coordinator at Grace United Methodist Church in Wautoma, Wisconsin. She also works as an assistant director at Lake Lucerne Camp and Retreat Center. Soozung enjoys coaching gymnastics and co-directing a community kids theatre production.

Acknowledgments

A big THANK YOU to these folks who care and know how to show it:

The youth at Grace UMC, Pastor Graham West, and Dawn DeBraal in Wautoma, Wisconsin

Youth leaders at Senior High Youth Convo '96, Madison, Wisconsin

Gretchen Fischer, Bridgewater, New Jersey

Danny Dixon, Grove City, Ohio

SKILLABILITIES FOR YOUTH WORKERS
Caring From the Inside Out:
How to Help Youth Show Compassion
Volume 3

SKILLABILITIES FOR YOUTH WORKERS, Vol. 3
(ISBN 0-687-06180-6) An official resource for The United Methodist Church prepared by The General Board of Discipleship through Teaching and Study Resources and published by Abingdon Press, The United Methodist Publishing House, 201 Eighth Avenue South, P.O. Box 801, Nashville, TN 37202-0801. Copyright © 1997 Abingdon Press All rights reserved. Printed in the United States of America.

To order copies of this publication, call 800-672-1789 from 7:00–6:30 (Central Time) Monday–Friday and 9–5:00 Saturday. Telecommunication Device for the Deaf/Telex Telephone: 800-227-4091. Automated order system is available after office hours.

For permission to reproduce any material in this publication, call 615-749-6421 or write to Permissions Office, 201 Eighth Avenue South, P.O. Box 801, Nashville, TN 37202-0801.

EDITORIAL AND DESIGN TEAM
Editor: Crystal A. Zinkiewicz
Production Editor: Susan Simmons
Design Manager: Phillip D. Francis
Designer: Diana Maio & Brooks Harper
Cover design: Diana Maio
& Phillip D. Francis

ADMINISTRATIVE TEAM
Publisher: Neil M. Alexander
Vice President: Harriett Jane Olson
Executive Editor, Teaching and Study Resources: Duane A. Ewers
Editor of Youth Resources: M. Steven Games

CONTENTS

WHY DO THIS?

Helping Youth Care From the Inside Out

SHORT-TERM BENEFITS

It's a crowd pleaser—
  People like to see that something is happening.

It's a crowd teaser—
  People will come back for more.

By-product:

Easy PR for your group,
 your church, and God.

Definitely sets you on **the right course**,
 even though it may be a baby step.

People like to see a project have
 a beginning and an ending.

Keeps the momentum going for the
 spiritually young and the spiritually
 mature all at the same time.

LONG-TERM BENEFITS

Youth become **grounded**
in the Scriptures.

You plant the **seeds** for lifelong
attitudes and skills of compassion.

These **roots** can grow strong and deep.

Transformation occurs.

Practicing how to care helps
build lasting friendships.

The skills of caring teach how
to nurture healthy relationships.

As youth care for others,

they also

build up

themselves.

Caring Builds Assets

Search Institute has identified **40 key assets** that make a difference in the quality of a young person's life now and later. Experiences of being cared about and of showing compassion and caring for others count!

CARING NEIGHBORHOOD **Asset #4**
Young person experiences caring neighbors.

CARING SCHOOL CLIMATE **Asset #5**
School provides a caring encouraging environment.

SERVICE TO OTHERS **Asset #9**
Young person serves in the community one hour or more per week.

CARING **Asset #26**
Young person places high value on helping other people.

Jesus
is the
perfect
example
of caring for
others.

Luke 4:16–21

Jesus defined his ministry in terms of caring:

- to bring good news to the poor.
- to proclaim release to captives and recovery to the blind.
- to let the oppressed go free.

The Gospels are filled with stories of Jesus' healing ministry. Later the disciples, filled with the Holy Spirit, were also able to heal. People experienced physical, emotional, and spiritual healing through the compassion of Jesus and his followers.

Mark 1:40–45

Jesus even healed people who were "untouchable," according to society. Those healed people in turn eagerly told others; they became great witnesses for Jesus and the caring that knowing him brings.

John 5:1–8

Jesus not only cared for the believers, but also for persons who had dug a hole for themselves and were stuck in a pity party that no one else would attend.

Jesus not only healed, but he also commanded this man to clean up his act—to take up his mat and walk and not to sin anymore.

Caring From the Inside Out

John 4:3–42

When it came to serving and doing God's work, Jesus wasn't concerned about his reputation. He associated with persons that society gossiped about and regarded as uncool and unwanted.

Matthew 9:35–10:1

Jesus had compassion for the people. He knew their needs. There was so much work to be done . . . so many people to help and to care for.

Caring From the Inside Out

Matthew 25:31–41
Romans 12:9–21

First **Jesus,**
and then **Paul,**
taught the people
who would follow
Jesus the Christ
the marks of
the **true Christian.**

What does the Lord

require of you

but to **do justice,**

and to **love kindness,**

and to **walk humbly**

with your God?

Micah 6:8

God's desire for people to care for one another and the creation is clear from the beginning.

However, you'll see with disappointment that even God's chosen leaders falter and sin; the people ignore the Law, which spelled out ways to care for one another. Repeatedly the prophets called them to repent, to turn again to the way of God: justice, kindness, relationship with the Most High.

We too falter and ignore what we know to be God's desire. But the Old Testament witness and God's saving grace in Jesus Christ reassures us. With God's help we too can care for persons—even with our faults and weaknesses—if we seek to be under God's authority.

WHAT'S THE CURRENT STATUS?

Ask Your Youth!

To whom would you give an award for caring?

Why?

TAKING OUR CARING PULSE

Caring for one another

How well do you think this group shows caring for each member? Circle the appropriate heart:

Do you remember a time with the group when you felt really cared for and cared about? Tell us about it.

Do you remember a time when you didn't feel the group cared, when you felt alone or left out or forgotten? Tell us about that too.

How can this group do better? List three activities or actions the group could try to improve the way we show caring for one another.

Caring beyond ourselves

How well do you think this group shows caring for people OUTSIDE its own members? Circle the appropriate heart:

What are three examples of individual behavior or of activities that this group could do to be more caring to others at school, in the community, or in the world?

Youth sometimes feel that adults assume youth are too young to know any better, that youth are not perceptive about what's going on around them, that they don't care. Rather, adults should

Assume brilliance!

—Craig McNair-Wilson,
nationally known speaker

Youth want to be treated as equals when it comes to making the world a more caring place. Adults need to assume that youth are mature enough to make a difference in lives around them. Adults need to assume that youth are capable.

Youth appreciate the guidance of positive adults who do not belittle them. Youth thrive on **mutual respect** and **trust.**

16 Ideas:
Youth to Youth;
Youth to Adults;
You to Youth

1 Prayer Partners

Have youth draw names of each other to be prayer partners for a month. Each month they draw different names. Then they can exchange phone numbers (even beeper numbers), so they can be in touch about prayer needs.

The partners may decide on specific times to stop what they are doing and pray for each other. For example, one may choose to pray at 4 p.m. wherever he or she is; another may claim the time for prayer while waiting for the bus.

2 Pal of the Month

Have the youth pick persons in the congregation they don't know very well. Use a church directory—especially a pictorial one—to identify people. Then for that month each youth is to do something caring for his or her secret pal. Or have one pal for the whole group to shower with attention.

Each month could have a theme:

HOMEBOUND PERSONS
COMMITTEE CHAIRPERSONS
SUNDAY SCHOOL TEACHERS
CHURCH EMPLOYEES
RETIRED FOLKS
YOUNG PARENTS
PARENTS OF TEENAGERS

You name it!

3 We're Cookin' Tonight

Youth can put on a dinner for their parents.

Choose a theme. For example, have the event around New Year's Day; encourage the making and sharing of New Year's resolutions that are visible signs of caring for each other.

4 Mail, Slightly Delayed

Right after the New Year, have youth draw names of people in the church youth group. Have them write a letter to that person at a youth group gathering. The letter should include words of praise, prayers for the year, and words of encouragement.

Give everyone envelopes to put the letters in and to address. Collect the letters, keep them in a safe spot, and mail them in a few months.

Send all the letters at Christmas time as a gift to one another. Send them individually for each person's birthday. Pick a time when not much is going on or pay attention to when difficult times happen for each young person and mail the letters then.

5 Thanks for the Memories

Sometime before November have each youth pick an adult they admire in the church (someone they are not related to). Give each teen a blank book.

The youth are to keep a journal of the person chosen, spending a few minutes each week writing down why they admire this person so much. If they see that their person appears in the paper, they can clip it out and paste it in the journal. If the youth finds a story or poem that is particularly nice, he or she can copy the story into the journal with a note after it saying why it was chosen. The entries that can be made are endless.

When Thanksgiving arrives, have the youth give the journal to the adult they chose.

6 Just Say Hi!

As a youth leader, make rounds to all the classes (12th grade and under) during Sunday school every once in awhile. Be sure to ask the Sunday school teachers ahead of time.

When visiting each class, present the same simple **challenge**:

Tell youth to stop that very day in the church and say "hi" to three adults they don't know.

Have you noticed that even in the church we get in the habit of ignoring each other because we don't know each other? These baby steps can help change that.

7 Hugs and Kisses

If the youth have an opportunity to do a children's sermon, do one about caring for one another. Even though they are working with the children, the message will reach the other youth and adults.

Bring large bags of Hershey Kisses and Hugs.™ Pass the bag around and have the children take 3-4 pieces. Send them down the aisles and tell them they must give away each piece to someone in the church they do not know very well. Call them all back and give them each a Hug and a Kiss for themselves.

This little gesture encourages taking risks with those in your own church family you don't know very well. It is also a quick but non-threatening way to symbolize reaching out across the generations.

8 Rah! Rah!

Be spontaneous. As a youth leader, call up a carload of youth and go to another youth's event at school. Teach youth to support each other at their programs, games, events, and other commitments. Cheers and applause from peers mean a lot.

9 Coffee? Tea? or "This Way, Please"

Have the youth sign up as hosts or greeters.

Youth can sign up to host one of the coffee hours Sunday morning if your church does this sort of thing. If your church does not regularly have a coffee hour, make this fellowship break a special occasion sponsored by the youth.

Youth can also sign up to be greeters Sunday morning at the entrance doors.

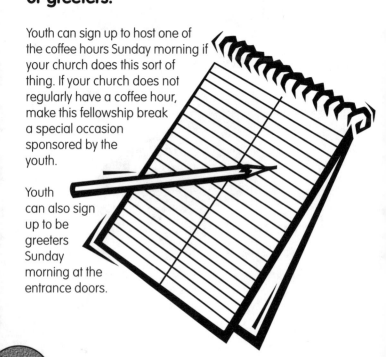

10 Treats

With a portion of the money your youth group has raised, **buy flowers** for some of the people who are homebound. Deliver the flowers in person or have them sent.

Spend one youth-gathering **making cookies** for homebound people or others who could use a "thinking of you" treat. Be sensitive to diets. If you are short on time and resources, use ready-made cookie batter. Deliver the cookies with a note, or spend a few minutes visiting.

Have a **BYOF—Bring Your Own Fruit**—youth group gathering. Put fruit baskets, boxes, or plates together to deliver to your chosen people.

Delivering treats doesn't have to be on holidays.

Do it just because.

11 Oops ...

**Being left out hurts—
even when it's unintentional.**

Make sure everyone knows what's going on and is able to attend. Have a list of the members; double-check arrangements with the group to make sure everyone is cared for.

Put in place a phone tree or ride-sharing plan among the active youth.

Then go on to the next step ...

32

12 Care Links

Pair an active youth with an inactive one. The active youth will be responsible for phoning the partner with information about what's going on, setting up rides, and telling him or her about any emergencies or special needs. Change the pairings each quarter.

In the youth room hang a chain of sturdy paper links. Use Velcro™ to fasten each circle. On each of the links write a youth's name. Include everyone, active and inactive. At each gathering of the group, unfasten the link of anyone not there. The broken chain illustrates the importance of each person's presence.

Be sure to celebrate any gathering whenever the chain is unbroken!

13 Hey! That's Me!

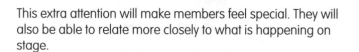

Do your youth perform skits and dramatic sketches in church for the worship service? Have them write their own scripts or adapt purchased ones to make the skits inclusive of the current experience and of the people in the church.

This extra attention will make members feel special. They will also be able to relate more closely to what is happening on stage.

14 Joys and Concerns

Create a ritual within the group for youth to share their highs and lows. Celebrate, give affirmations. Listen, show empathy.

Pray together —

giving thanks to God

for the joys,

asking for God to

deal with the concerns

and **give strength,**

peace, and **guidance**

as needed.

15 Show Them You Care

Get yourself some fun stationery or letterhead. Drop a note or make a quick phone call to the various youth in your church. Just say "Hi" or "Thank you" or how much you appreciate their presence.

Do the same for adults, as individuals or as a group, who do something nice for your youth. Also encourage your youth to respond with a quick note or card of thanks. Together you will be creating a more caring church community.

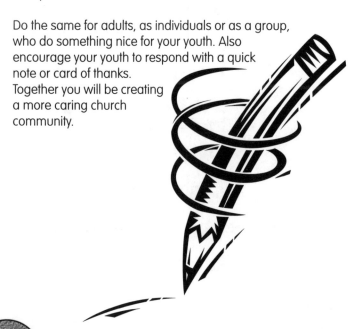

16 Beep, Beep

One of the best ways to show caring is by being available, listening, and praying. Consider carrying a prayer pager. Create a business card to give to each of your youth. Include on the card the beeper number and a series of codes for the youth to use to communicate their need to you. Laminate the card to make it last longer. Encourage the youth to share the card with others who want someone to pray for them.

From <u>YouthNet</u>, Volume 4, Number 1, page 5.

Danny's Prayer Pager 555-3054

When you hear the tone—
- Enter your code number
- Press the star (*) button
- Enter the code of your prayer request (listed on other side)
- Press the pound (#) button when done.
- If you'd like me to call you, after your code number enter the phone number where I can reach you.

Prayer Concern Codes

1 Test today	**8** Boyfriend problems
2 Game today	**9** Girlfriend problems
3 Competition	**10** Problem with dad
4 School problem	**11** Problem with mom
5 Better grades	**12** Problem with sister
6 Witnessing opportunity	**13** Problem with brother
7 I'm sick	**14** PANIC! I need help

13
Fun
&
Nifty
Ideas

1 Make a New Friend

Help your youth to be on the lookout for other teens who seem to have no one. Into your ongoing group times, incorporate practice sessions on how to be friendly, how to invite people to church-related activities, and how to make new people feel welcome.

Practice sessions do two things:

They reinforce the need to reach out and care for other youth—especially the loners—and give youth the skills needed to be able to follow through with their good intentions.

Adapted from YouthNet, Volume 3, Number 4.

2 Practice Random Acts of Kindness

Save the tubes from toilet tissue and paper towel rolls. Fill them with candies, messages, and other small spirit-lifters. Gift wrap them, leaving the paper extended over the ends. Tie each end with a ribbon.

THEN LET THE FUN BEGIN.

Go someplace and randomly pass out your gifts —
and watch
the **smiles**
appear!

3 "Hi, I'm Jack"

Carve pumpkins in the fall for persons in the hospital. Deliver your jack o' lanterns to those you do not know at all.

Ask the hospital nurses to indicate which patients haven't had many visitors or could use an extra lift.

Early in the Christmas season, deliver poinsettias to persons in the hospital. Use money raised by the youth; add a message of God's love.

4 Christmas-Smiles Deliveries

Ask the youth if they know of any peers at school who are living without any luxuries most of the time. **Load a pick-up truck with Christmas trees** that the youth cut themselves or bought with money they've raised. Deliver the trees to their schoolmates' homes the weekend before Thanksgiving. Then the families can walk into the holiday season with smiles on their faces.

5 Pets and Small Children

Bring friendly pets from your youth's families to visit a nursing home, retirement home, or care center. Pets have a way of bringing out the best in people. Be sure to ask the center and especially each person for permission in advance.

Or have your youth **bring along younger brothers or sisters**. Small children have the same positive effect as friendly animals. They have a way of tugging at the heartstrings and bringing cheer.

6 Celebrate Together

Have the youth **organize a multicultural party or fair**. Hold it at a school for the community. Working together with youth of other cultures is a positive and fun thing to do. The celebration promotes understanding and cultivates an appreciation for differences. It also helps people recognize the similarities that bring us together. These benefits occur not only across cultures but also within cultures.

From <u>Party: Invitation to the Reign of God</u>, Leader's Guide (Cokesbury), pages 18–21.

7 On a Mission From God

Any kind of mission trip—local, out-of-town, out-of-state, out-of-country—is a way to put caring into action. There are many different organizations to go through. If it's the first time you've planned such a trip, **link up with a church that has gone on a mission trip in the past**. Learn from them before you dive into doing one yourself. Most churches will welcome the partnership.

8 Care Packages

If you aren't ready for a mission trip, then consider putting together care packages. Send the packages to your mission country (ask your church missions committee) or send them to missionary families who are ministering to those far away.

Often missionaries go afield with their entire family. Find out the ages of the children and teenagers and send a care package specifically for them.

If you're ready for more, then consider this idea!

Send a larger care package for the missionary families to use for the children and youth they come in contact with in the mission field.

9 Serving Up Love

Schedule regular trips to a local soup kitchen and assist in serving meals. **Begin thinking of how your youth can do more than just serve meals.**

Think of ways to help the homeless get back on their feet and become independent again. Work with a local agency to see what is needed to eliminate this problem of homelessness.

Consider filling backpacks with small personal-care items, like toothbrush, soap, tissue, and socks, to give to people in need.

10 Creation Caring

**Help the environment. Plant trees.
Clean up a creek bed. Adopt a highway or
street. Create a garden.**

Look especially in depressed areas of your
community. Whatever the group does to care for
the environment is also caring for the people who
live there.

Take care of a garden or yard for an older adult
who can no longer do so.

From _Beyond Leaf Raking_, by Benson and Roehlkepartain (Abingdon Press, 1993).

11 What Goes Around Comes Around

Use recycled or recyclable paper to make home-made paper. Go to a craft or nature store and pick up a paper-making kit. Your youth will have fun re-creating paper in their own way.

Have the youth send notes on recycled paper to local businesses, congratulating them on their efforts to recycle. Offer to assist the businesses by picking up aluminum cans.

Youth may use the profits to update and upgrade recycling areas in the community, especially in public areas.

If your community does not have a recycling program, the youth may want to campaign to get something established for the sake of the earth.

12 A Beary Merry Christmas

At Christmas time set up a tree in the church to collect teddy bears. Put the larger ones under the tree and hang the smaller ones on the tree. After Christmas donate the bears to a children's cause; there are many out there.

From <u>Interpreter</u>, October 1996

13 Back to School

Call the principals of your community schools. Ask them if you may eat with the students from your church at lunch. Call the group the Lunch Bunch. Eventually you will be surrounded by their friends, some of whom will be unchurched. Get to know them as well. As you do acts of caring for your youth, include their friends. Model caring.

The Lunch Bunch may lead to youth-led Bible studies in school or to more youth coming to church and youth functions.

School counselors may welcome your presence. Connect with them; see where you can be used. You may find a special role as a classroom tutor. Your extra hands are a relief to teachers who need a boost of positive energy and leadership. Show your caring for the community, the school, and the teachers, as well as for the youth.

Attitudes, Skills, and Actions

To go out into the church

or community with

an attitude of caring yourself ...

Stay **focused on Jesus**
and his caring ways.

Little Things Count

Make a list of the people who made a difference in your life as a teenager. Next to each name jot down the types of conversations the two of you had. Add some examples of the caring things you did for one another. Note them even if they were simply saying "thank you" or doing something that lifted the other person's spirits.

Remember and

give thanks

for these small acts

as you empower

your youth

to do the same.

Practice What You Preach

Affirm your youth for the caring they already show. But help them be more intentional about it. Here are some skills that are important. Invite the youth to make up some roleplays or skits to illustrate using these skills.

Practice . . .

. . . recognizing the moods of others:

- Notice the situation that is occurring.

- Note the other person's facial expressions, voice tone, and gestures.

- Think about what feelings you are experiencing when you demonstrate similar behaviors.

- Assess the other person's current mood or feelings.

- If possible, check out your assessment with him or her. "It seems to me that you are _____. Is that the case?"

The skills given above are from Teaching Social Skills to Youth, by Tom Dowd and Jeff Tierney (BoysTown Press, 1992). Used with permission.

. . . responding with empathy and understanding:

- Listen closely and give your full attention to the other person.

- Acknowledge what he or she is saying and feeling: "You're feeling _____." "What I heard you say was _____."

- Demonstrate concern through words: "That's too bad." "No wonder you're upset."

- Demonstrate caring through actions. Give a hug. Get or do something that's needed. Send a follow-up note or card. Help the other person think of alternatives. (You do not have to solve or fix the problem; your role is to be supportive.)

- Encourage the person to seek more help if necessary.

The skills given above are from <u>Teaching Social Skills to Youth</u>, by Tom Dowd and Jeff Tierney (BoysTown Press, 1992). Used with permission.

Walk a Mile in Someone Else's Moccasins

Invite a person with disabilities to talk to the youth. The focus can be on appropriate and inappropriate ways of relating to people with handicapping conditions. What acts of compassion are helpful? What ways of expressing compassion are not appreciated?

Think of situations; do some roleplaying. Allow the person with disabilities to give the youth affirmation or suggestions of alternatives that would be more helpful.

Make Caring Visible

Use a bulletin board or newsletter. Post photos of "caring in action" and other notes or clippings that show what youth have done for others. Also include information about upcoming opportunities.

Encourage the pastor to affirm the youth. **A word of thanks from the pulpit is great.** A one-to-one compliment helps a youth feel valued.

CARING IN ACTION

Thank You for Caring

Set Your Own Priorities

Spend some

intentional time

on caring for yourself . . .

and your relationship

with God.

By doing so you can continue to teach others how to care. If you lose perspective on the importance of this element of caring, so will others.

CARING ACCORDING TO PAUL

Instructions from the Letter to the Romans, a Bible Study for youth.

> "Let love be genuine; hate what is evil, hold fast to what is good . . ."
>
> Romans 12:9

Compassion needs to extend beyond simple acts of kindness. When evil is present, Christians are called to seek justice.

- Think together. Where is there evil at work? What issues, what systems, what practices are harming people? They may be in school, in the community, or in the world.

- What can youth do? Focus attention on the problem? (Speak out, write letters, lobby, boycott, produce a video, make a presentation?)

- Who is already working on the issue? What energy, skills, people-power can the youth add? (Stuffing envelopes, distributing flyers, collecting signatures?)

"Contribute to the needs of the saints . . ."

Romans 12:13a

Take care of other Christians. What are their needs? Consider their personal needs, but also think of ways to contribute to the needs of their ministry. All Christians are called to be in ministry. How can we support one another as we minister to others?

" . . . extend hospitality to strangers."

Romans 12:13b

Caring is not just for people we know or for people who are like us. It is also for those we do not know or who are different from us. To extend hospitality is to welcome people, to make them feel comfortable, to care for their physical needs, and to keep them safe while they are in your care.

"Rejoice with those who rejoice . . ."

Romans 12:15a

Caring is sharing—sharing in the happy times as well as the hurting ones. But jealousy can mar happy times. Susan got the dream guy, job, college, gift, award. Be happy for her and with her. Show her you care. Participate in her joy. When your turn for rejoicing comes, your happiness will be greater for having persons celebrate for and with you.

". . . weep with those who weep."

Romans 12:15b

Empathy is feeling with someone else. When death or disaster strikes, no matter how much you care, you may not be able to change anything. Caring is sometimes simply being present with someone who is hurting.

"My friends were there for me. I know they care about me."

"Do not be haughty, but associate with the lowly . . ."

Romans 9:16b

Don't think you are better than others. Look through God's eyes: All persons—no matter how society labels them—are persons of worth. You and they are both children of God. When you serve others—when you relate to others—treat them with respect. Honor their dignity. That's another way of showing your caring.

" 'If your enemies are hungry, feed them; if they are thirsty, give them something to drink . . . ' Overcome evil with good."

Romans 12:20–21

Your caring acts—however hard to do—will surprise the ones who would see you as an enemy. Evil will not get the best of you.

<u>Here's an assignment</u>: Think of one person you dislike or who dislikes you for some reason. Resolve to do something special for him or her (a note, a smile, a candy bar). See if your caring can change a foe into a friend, evil into good.

Do you "Assume brilliance"?

Caring From the Inside Out

Do your youth seem apathetic or uncaring?

- Talk about caring. Make it important.
- Study the Bible together.
- Do roleplays and practice the skills.
- Shower them with caring.
- Challenge them to compassion actions—
  then they will begin to feel caring.

Do you show your caring?

Do your other adult workers seem unwilling or unable to take the lead in a compassion action?

Start small. Select one idea and ask someone else to see it through. Involve the persons in the selection if possible. Give them a small project that is nonthreatening and simple. Nothing is simple, right?

Choose your help **prayerfully.**
Select your idea **carefully.**

Give them a chance to struggle through it—with your support. This is how you grow leaders.

Adults need just as much self-esteem building as youth. Help them feel competent. Affirm their efforts.

"ASSUME BRILLIANCE!" If you don't, you may burn out trying to do everything yourself. Be patient and build for the future.

Working With Difficult Persons

What would **Jesus** do this very moment in this **situation** with this difficult person?

How to Be Effective and Compassionate!

If your helper is just plain childish and bringing out the worst in everyone else, ask the helper to use his or her gifts in another area of the church or youth group. In such situations, focus on the idea of what the person's gifts are and the best use for them. He or she may be gifted in doing the "behind the scenes" work that is also necessary for youth ministry to succeed.

If your helper is a poor role model, confront him or her about specific actions. This approach does not attack the person, but the behavior.

If your helper is abusive (emotionally, spiritually), then confront him or her with support from and along with another leader from your church whom you trust. As best you can, see that the person gets some help. But remove him or her from working with youth.

Tough love can heal not only your pain but also his or hers. This confrontation could be a turning point for this person.

Your youth are

watching you.

How you handle

difficult persons is

a test.

You have the

opportunity

to model actions that

are Christ-like. You

will be showing

compassion in

action.

Mini-WorkShop

FOR LEADERS

minutes

- WELCOME ACTIVITY   5–15

—Share with one another personal experiences of being cared for.

- BIBLE STUDY (pages 9–17)   10–15

—From the passages list traits of caring.

- WHAT'S THE CURRENT STATUS? (pages 18–21)   10–15

—Try out the assessment tools.

- GETTING THE BIG PICTURE (pages 71–72, 8)   5–10

—Define ethos and examine its role; look at the assets.

- CREATING AN ETHOS OF CARING (pages 22–51)   15–25

—In smaller groups review the ideas and add more.

- HOW TO HELP YOUTH SHOW COMPASSION   15–25
  (pages 54–59)

—Choose some compassion actions to begin with; do roleplays and practice skills (pages 54–56).

- CLOSING   5

—Read aloud Romans 12:9–21; pray together.

70

Caring From the Inside Out

THE BIG PICTURE

Working with youth is a little like putting together a jigsaw puzzle: It helps to have a picture of what it's supposed to look like! (See page 73.)

In effective youth ministry **vision** is central.

Seven major elements contribute to realizing that vision. The more of them developed and in place, the better.

Youth ministry planners in individual churches can develop each of those areas **their own way,** according to their congregation's particular resources, gifts, and priorities and the needs of their youth.

How does this SkillAbility fit in this big picture? Here are just a few of the ways. By using ideas in this book, not only do you help youth show compassion, you also

• create an **ETHOS** around caring, which gives the group an identity that is distinctively Christian.

• create **STRUCTURE** that facilitates communication and outreach to connect young people to a caring group.

• increase teenagers' **EXPERIENCES** of living the Word and following the example of Jesus, through kindness, justice, and care for creation.

• forge bonds between youth and adults in the **CONGREGATION,** which then communicate to young people they are valued and cared for.

• send youth into the **COMMUNITY** as servants caring for persons in need and as witnesses to the love and reign of God.

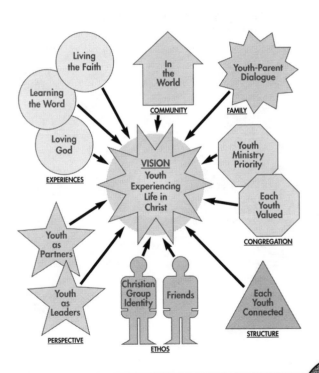

YOUTH MINISTRY: A COMPREHENSIVE APPROACH

Living the Faith

Learning the Word

Loving God

EXPERIENCES

In the World

COMMUNITY

Youth-Parent Dialogue

FAMILY

VISION Youth Experiencing Life in Christ

Youth Ministry Priority

Each Youth Valued

CONGREGATION

Youth as Partners

Youth as Leaders

PERSPECTIVE

Christian Group Identity

Friends

ETHOS

Each Youth Connected

STRUCTURE

FAMILY

Research is clear that **parent-youth dialogue** about matters of faith are crucial for youth to develop mature faith. Youth themselves express desire to be listened to, to have boundaries, and to have parental involvement in their lives. Parents need skills for relating to their changing teens as well as assurance that their values and voice do matter to their youth. How do we in the church facilitate parent-youth dialogue?

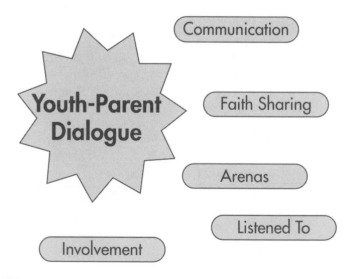

Communication

Youth-Parent Dialogue

Faith Sharing

Arenas

Listened To

Involvement

CONGREGATION

Youth ministry is the ministry of the whole congregation, beginning with making **youth ministry a priority**: prayer for the ministry, people (not just one person!), time, effort, training, resources, and funding. The goal for the congregation is **each youth valued**. Interaction with adults, including mentors, positive language about youth, prayer partners for each one, simply being paid attention to—these are active roles for the congregation.

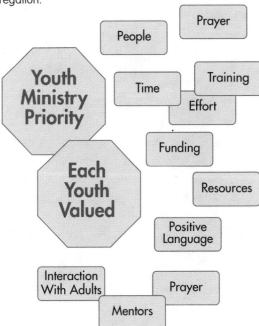

STRUCTURE

Whatever shape the ministry takes, the goal is to have **each youth connected.** Sunday school and youth group are only a beginning. What are the needs of the youth? What groups (even of 2 or 3), what times would help connect young people to the faith community? How easy is it for new youth to enter? How well do we stay in touch with the changing needs of our youth? Do we have structures in place that facilitate communication? outreach? "How" can vary; it's the "why" that's crucial.

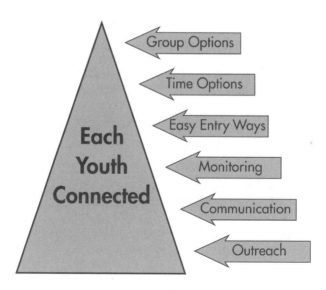

Group Options

Time Options

Easy Entry Ways

Monitoring

Communication

Outreach

Each Youth Connected

ETHOS

We are relational beings; we all need **friends**. The support, caring, and accountability friends provide help youth experience the love of God. As those friendships are nurtured within **Christian group identity**, young people claim for themselves a personal identity of being Christian. What language, rituals, traditions, and bonding experiences mark each grouping within the youth ministry as distinctively Christian?

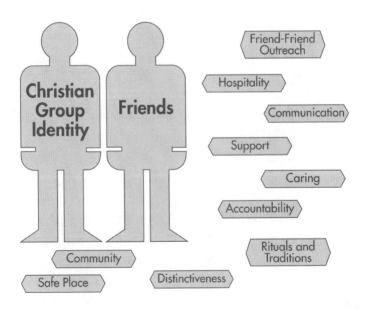

Christian Group Identity

Friends

Friend-Friend Outreach

Hospitality

Communication

Support

Caring

Accountability

Rituals and Traditions

Community

Safe Place

Distinctiveness

PERSPECTIVE

Youth are keenly aware of being seen as problems, being treated as objects to be fixed, or as recipients too inexperienced to have anything to offer. What would happen if we operated from the perspective of seeing **youth as leaders, youth as partners**? We would listen to them more, be intentional about identifying their gifts, take seriously their input, encourage their decision making, and train them for leadership roles.

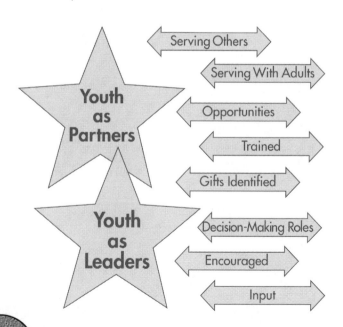

EXPERIENCES

Worship, devotions, prayer, and participation in the community of faith build for youth the experience of **loving God**. Study and reflection upon the Bible and the faith are crucial for **learning the Word**. Being among people who are Christian role models and grappling with difficult moral, ethical, justice, and stewardship issues help young people with **living the faith**. Curriculum resources specifically provide material to facilitate these three kinds of experiences.

COMMUNITY

As Christians, youth are challenged to be **in the world** as servants, as witnesses, as leaven—making a difference with their lives, giving others a glimpse of the Kingdom. What opportunities, what training, what support do we give youth to equip them for ministry beyond the walls of the church building?

In the World

Serving

Witnessing

Leaven/Salt/Light